My Sticker Paintings

PETS

PARAKEET

JACK RUSSELL
TERRIER

TORTOISE

PONY

ROOSTER

CAT

CANARY

HUSKY

GOLDFISH

RABBIT

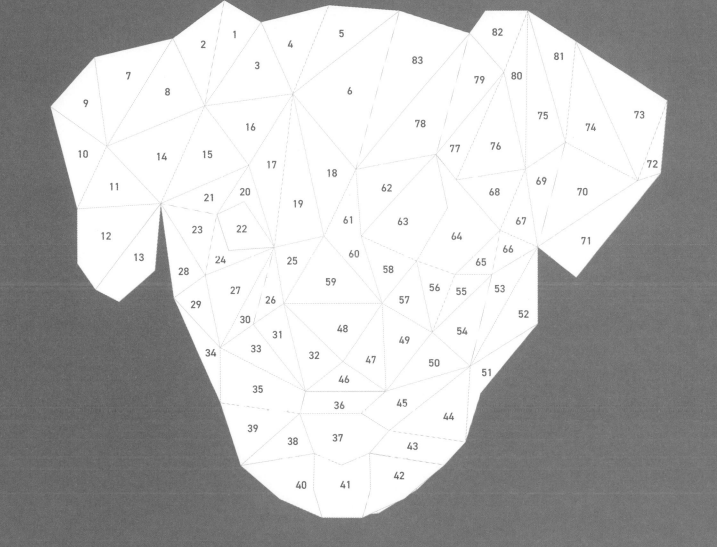

JACK RUSSELL TERRIER

BABY: Puppy

SIZE: 12–14 inches long

WEIGHT: 14–18 pounds

FOOD: Kibble and meat

LIFESPAN: 13–16 years

Did you know?

The Jack Russell Terrier is a great jumper. It can jump up to 5 feet high!

The Jack Russell Terrier is a smart, active, and lively dog. It was originally a hunting dog, so it is naturally fast, curious, and has lots of energy. It is also a fast learner, making it easy to train, and is a wonderful family pet.

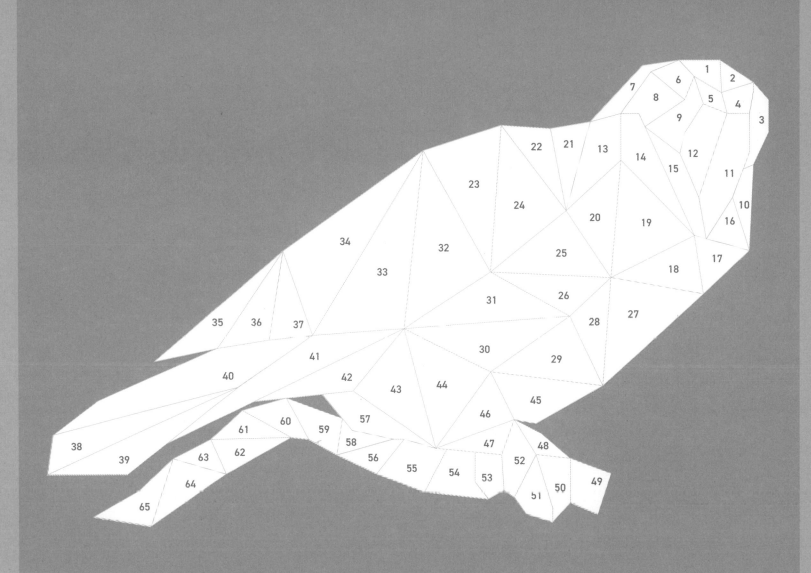

PARAKEET

PARAKEET

SIZE: 7–10 inches

WEIGHT: 1–1.6 ounces

FOOD: Seeds, fruit, and vegetables

LIFESPAN: 10–15 years

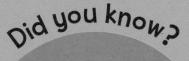

Did you know?

Parakeets don't like being alone. They need the company of another parakeet or a person to keep them happy and mentally stimulated.

This little parakeet originated in Australia and is known for its colorful plumage and chirping.
Parakeets also love contact with humans.
Once it trusts you, it likes to fly around the room and peck seeds out of your hand
before returning to its perch.

PONY

PONY

KEY INFO

FEMALE: Mare

BABY: Foal

SIZE: 2.6–4.8 feet at its shoulders

WEIGHT: 330–660 pounds

FOOD: Hay, straw, cereal, and vegetation

LIFESPAN: 30–40 years

Did you know?

Ponies and horses are measured by hand lengths from shoulder to foot. (A hand is about 4 inches, and the number after the decimal is the inches left over from the hand.) A pony is smaller than 14.2 hands.

From tiny Shetlands to large ponies, each child can find one to suit his or her size and go for a ride. Ponies need a large meadow to graze in, a hut for shelter, and a friend (another pony, a donkey, or a goat), because they hate being on their own.

ROOSTER

ROOSTER

FEMALE: Hen

BABY: Chick

SIZE: 12–22 inches

WEIGHT: 1.8–11 pounds

FOOD: Seeds, worms, and insects

LIFESPAN: 10–12 years

Did you know?

To lay eggs, a hen needs 12 hours of daylight per day. It lays an egg every day and eats 330 pounds of kitchen and garden waste per year.

With its "cocorico"—its red crest—and its large feathers, the rooster is the king of the henhouse. Chickens are not affectionate like cats or dogs, but they are very quick to recognize the people who care for them.

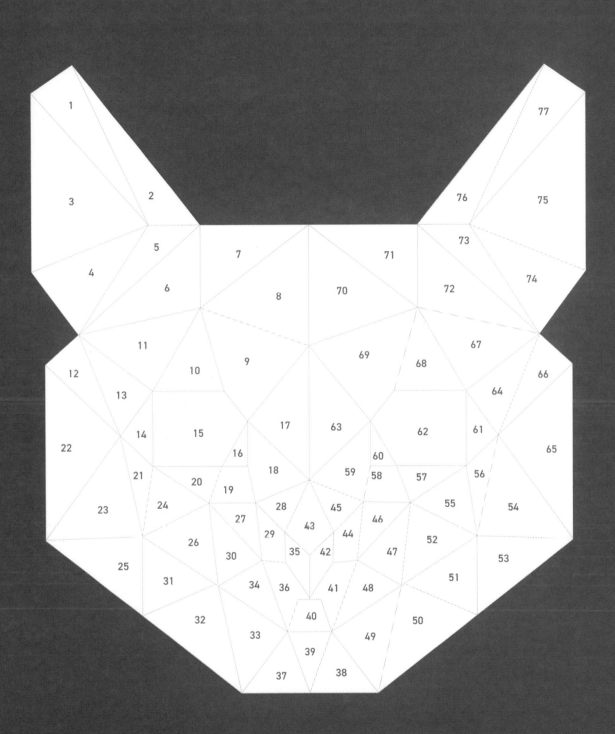

CAT

CAT

BABY: Kitten

SIZE: 26–30 inches, including its tail

WEIGHT: 5.5–11 pounds

FOOD: Kibble, small rodents, and birds

LIFESPAN: 15–18 years

Did you know?

Thanks to their extraordinary flexibility and sense of balance, cats almost always land on their feet.

Cats love to play with small objects. Being independent, though, they are the ones who decide when it's time to play. When they are happy, they purr and retract their claws to play, which some call "velvet paws."

GOLDFISH

GOLDFISH

KEY INFO

BABY: Fry
SIZE: 8–12 inches
WEIGHT: 0.4–3.3 pounds
FOOD: Flakes or pellets
LIFESPAN: 8–10 years

Did you know?

Despite their name, goldfish can be red, black, white, and yellow in addition to gold (or orange).

Goldfish are peaceful and easy pets to care for.
They need a big bowl of water
and a few plants. A companion helps
them feel less lonely and they may even kiss each other.
They should be fed a very small amount twice a day
and have their water changed every week.

RABBIT

RABBIT

Did you know?

A rabbit's teeth continue growing throughout its entire life. It wears them down by constantly nibbling.

As a pet, rabbits are calm and affectionate, and love to be cuddled. Once they get used to their litter box, they can be allowed to roam around the house. Whenever they sense danger, they thump the ground with one of their hind legs and take refuge in their burrow.

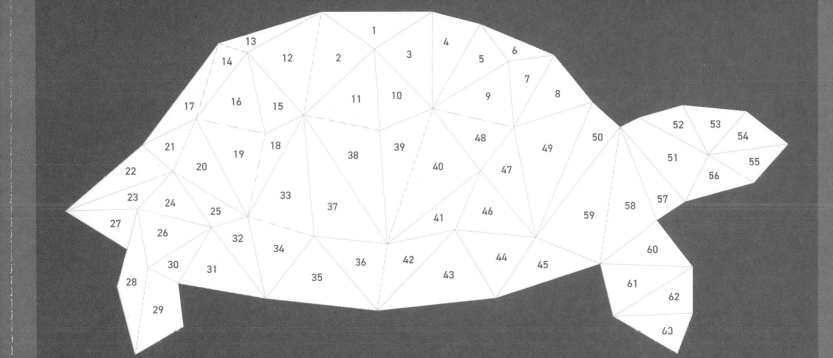

TORTOISE

TORTOISE

SIZE: 8–12 inches

WEIGHT: 6.6–8.8 pounds

FOOD: Plants, vegetables, fruit, and insects

LIFESPAN: 50–100 years

Did you know?

A tortoise hibernates from about November to March. To protect itself from the cold, it buries itself and tucks its head and legs into its shell.

A tortoise is a wild animal that sometimes lives in gardens. Because of its short legs and the weight of its shell, it moves very slowly. It is not the ideal pet for indoors, and it doesn't enjoy playing or cuddling very much. Instead, it enjoys sunshine and fresh air.

CANARY

KEY INFO

SIZE: 4–8 inches
WEIGHT: 0.5–1 ounce
FOOD: Cereal and fruit
LIFESPAN: 8–10 years

Did you know?

To sleep, a canary will perch on one leg and tuck its beak and head into its feathers.

This small yellow bird is native to the Canary Islands and is known for its melodious song. The canary is a cheerful companion whose good humor is contagious. It doesn't like being alone and enjoys the company of other small birds. It is the most popular pet bird.

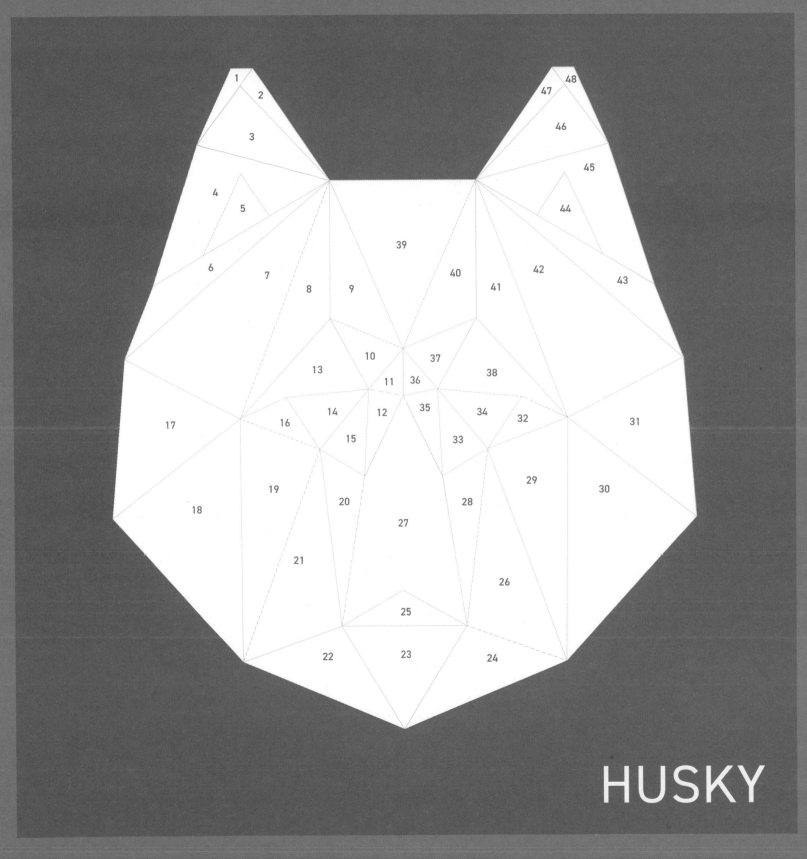

HUSKY

HUSKY

BABY: Puppy

SIZE: 1.6–2 feet at its shoulders

WEIGHT: 35–60 pounds

FOOD: Kibble and meat

LIFESPAN: 12–15 years

Did you know?

Many huskies have two blue eyes, while some can even be born with one blue eye and one brown eye.

In its native Siberia, as in other regions around the poles, a husky is used to pull sleds on the snow. It is fast and has a lot of stamina, with a great love of the outdoors and the need to let off steam in the wild. A husky is a good-natured and people-loving pet.

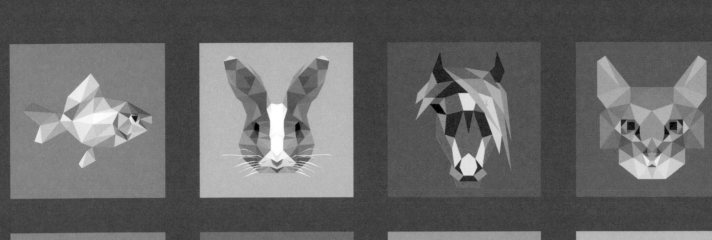

STICKERS

JACK RUSSELL TERRIER

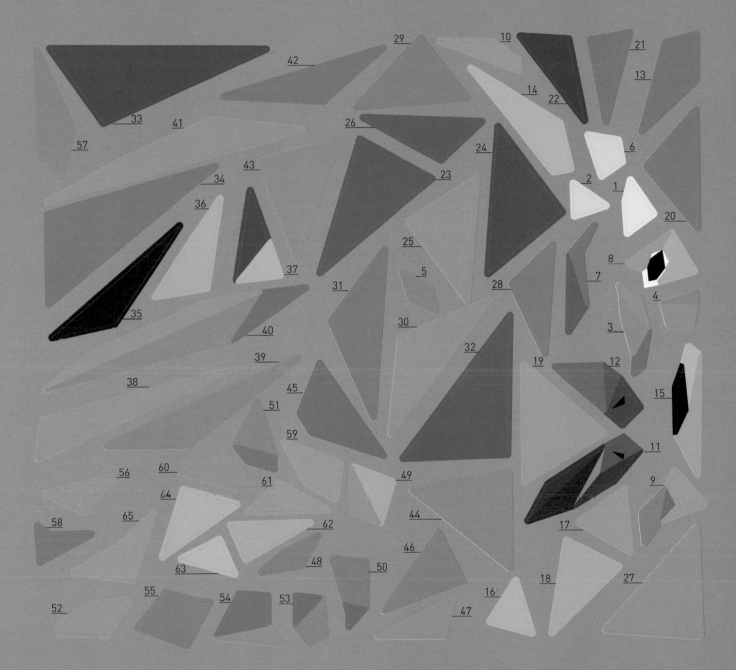

PARAKEET

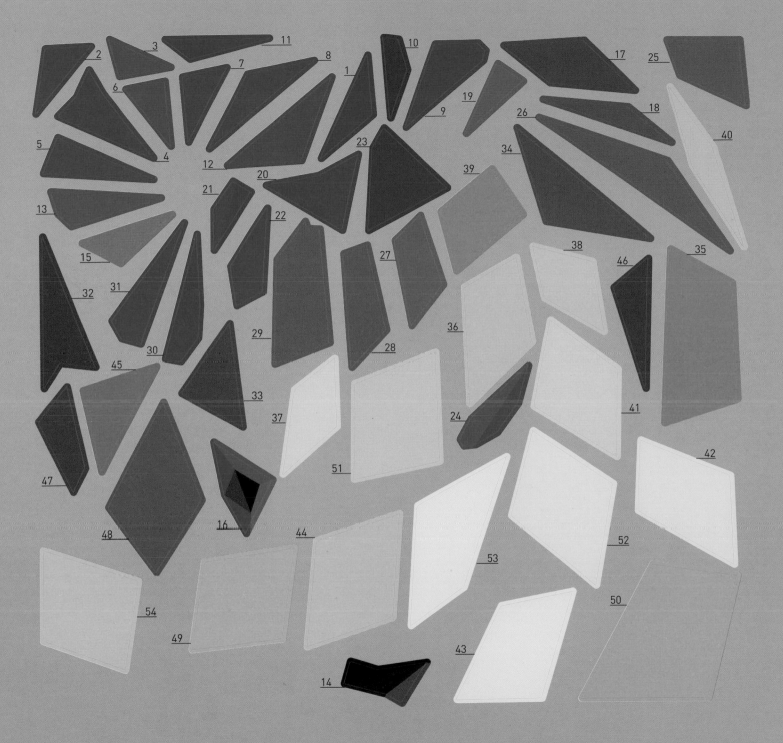

ROOSTER

CAT

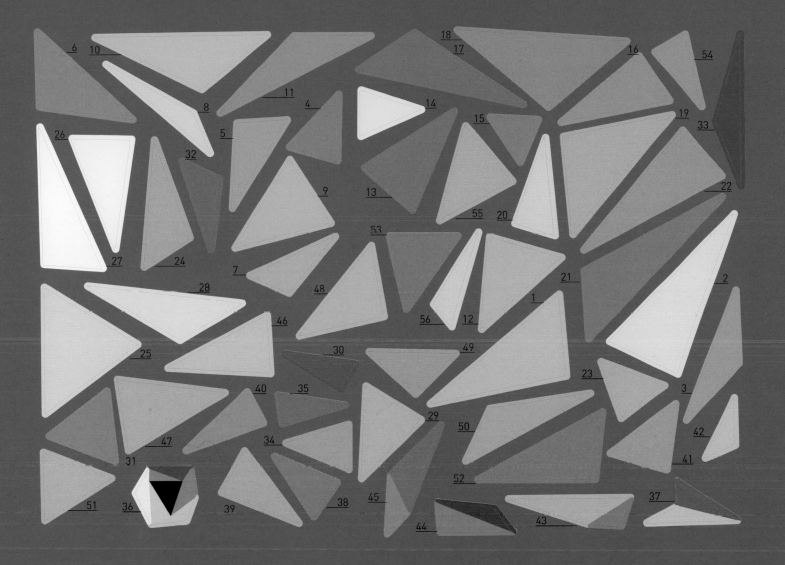

GOLDFISH

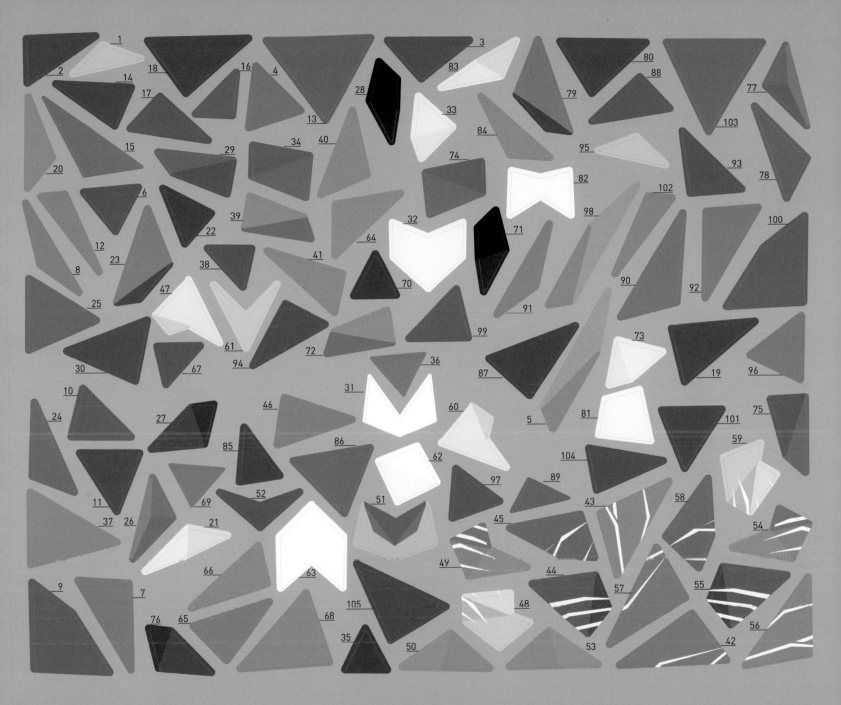

RABBIT

TORTOISE

CANARY

HUSKY